Editor
Sara Connolly

Cover Artist
Denise Bauer

Editor in Chief
Ina Massler Levin, M.A.

Creative Director
Karen J. Goldfluss, M.S. Ed.

Art Coordinator
Renée Christine Yates

Imaging
James Edward Grace

BUILDING WRITING SKILLS
Grades 3–4

Paragraphs to Stories

Includes Standards & Benchmarks

Learn to organize a paragraph and structure a story.

Discover how to write for a specific audience.

Explore purpose for writing a story.

Publish completed stories with illustrations.

One day Mr. Sully invited Jason to visit a humane society with him. He needed help and Jason was willing to go. Jason helped Mr. Sully clean the cages and feed dogs. He took animals out into the yard. He enjoyed being with the dog and playing with them.

Publisher
Mary D. Smith, M.S. Ed.

Author

Tracie I. Heskett, M.Ed.

Teacher Created Resources, Inc.
12621 Western Avenue
Garden Grove, CA 92841
www.teachercreated.com
ISBN: 978-1-4206-3940-1
©2... ..., Inc.

D1416370

Teacher Created Resources

Table of Contents

Introduction

When writing is considered an important component of the reading process, amazing things can happen. Writing, after all, is the expression of things learned. It is an active process when students are allowed to discover, reflect, and create. Higher-order thinking skills are awakened as students analyze, synthesize, construct meaning, and make connections through use of the written word. Research has shown that reading and writing are co-dependent and one cannot exist to full potential without the other; both reading and writing facilitate each other. For students to benefit from the writing process, effective writing strategies should be introduced and practiced. Writing strategies will allow students to expand the natural thinking process and transform that thinking into written words.

In *Paragraphs to Stories*, students learn how to use paragraphs to develop ideas and write complete stories. Students learn basic concepts related to writing stories, including definitions of different types of stories and the process of writing a story. Students will also learn about audience and purpose for their writing. Lessons introduce key story elements, such as characters, setting, plot, suspense, and mood, as well as the "show, don't tell" technique in writing.

Students will practice mapping out a story and learn how to make a story seem as if it really could happen. Editing practice is provided as students choose a story to edit. They will include illustrations with their work and consider publishing options. The teacher resource section includes suggestions for publishing student work.

Several lessons suggest generating a class chart for student reference throughout the activities. You may wish to predetermine a consistent format for these charts, such as flip charts on an interactive whiteboard or chart paper, posters to display in the classroom, or individual copies that students can keep in a notebook.

List of Charts

- Story Types (Genres) (student-generated)

- A Complete Story (optional for classroom display)

- Combined Class Categories Game Card

- Characters Feel . . . Characters Act

- Show, Don't Tell Triangle

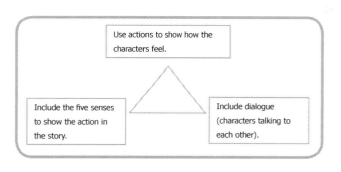

You may wish to have students keep their work—paragraphs and stories, graphic organizers, and other activity pages, etc.—in portfolios to refer to throughout the lessons. Students will select one or more stories to edit and illustrate for publication.

Standards

The lessons in *Paragraphs to Stories* meet the following writing standards, which are used with permission from McREL.

McREL, Mid–continent Research for Education and Learning, ©2009.

http://www.mcrel.org Telephone: (303) 337–0990

Standard	Pages
1.1 Use prewriting strategies to plan written work (e.g., uses story maps)	11, 13–15, 17–18, 38–39, 42
1.2 Uses strategies to draft and revise written work (e.g., elaborates on a central idea)	5, 24, 25–26, 35–36, 38–39
1.3 Uses strategies to publish written work (e.g., considers page format (paragraphs, margins, indentations, titles); selects presentation format according to purpose; incorporates photos, illustrations; uses available technology to compose and publish work)	42–43, 45–46
1.4 Evaluates own and others' writing (e.g., asks for feedback; responds to classmates' writing)	17–18, 24, 31–32
1.5 Uses strategies (e.g., adapts focus, determines interests of audience) to write for different audiences (e.g., peers)	7
1.6 Uses strategies (e.g., adapts focus) to write for a variety of purposes (e.g., to inform, entertain, explain, describe, record ideas)	8–9
1.8 Writes narrative accounts, such as poems and stories (e.g., creates an organizing structure; sequences events, develops characters, setting, and plot; creates an organizing structure; sequences events; uses concrete sensory details)	17–18, 21–22, 24, 25–26, 27–28, 31–32, 33, 35–36, 38–39, 41, 42
1.10 Writes expressive compositions (e.g., expresses ideas, reflections, and observations; uses an individual, authentic voice; uses narrative strategies, relevant details, and ideas that enable the reader to imagine the world of the event or experience)	21–22, 33, 35–36, 42
2.1 Uses descriptive language that clarifies and enhances ideas (e.g., sensory details)	25–26
2.2 Uses paragraph form in writing (e.g., uses an introductory and concluding paragraph, writes several related paragraphs)	25–26, 41
2.3 Uses a variety of sentence structures in writing (e.g., expands basic sentence patterns, uses exclamatory or imperative sentences)	41
3 Uses grammatical and mechanical conventions in written compositions	42–43
3.4 Uses verbs in written compositions (e.g., uses a wide variety of action verbs, past and present verb tenses)	21–22

Stories Around Us

Objective

Using samples of stories, students will create a chart listing characteristics or features of stories and will retell stories in their own words.

Materials

- "What is a Story?" page 6, one copy per student
- copy of a modified fairy tale, such as *The Three Little Javelinas* (Susan Lowell, Scholastic, 1992)

Opening

1. Distribute copies of "What is a Story?"

2. Have students check any statements they think define a story.

3. Discuss the statements together as a class to arrive at a working definition of a story.

Directions

1. Have students consider their favorite classroom (story) books. Ask them to think about what they notice about the stories. As time allows, have student volunteers read story excerpts, or display a page from a picture book.

2. As a class, create a "What We Notice About Stories" chart similar to the one below.

What We Notice About Stories

- A story has more than one character.
- The main character has a problem to solve, an obstacle to overcome, or a situation to work through.
- A story tells what happens to the characters.
- We can identify when and where a story takes place.
- The characters have thoughts and feelings.
- There is action in a story.
- The characters talk to each other.

Closing

1. Have students select short stories that they particularly enjoy. They will "
   thinking of similar stories. Explain that "mimic" means to imitate or co

2. Demonstrate by discussing a well-known fairy tale that has been rew
   Javelinas. Discuss how this story incorporates the characteristics l

3. Encourage students to think of their own characters, settings, an'
   stories similar to the short stories they selected. Have them tel'

#3249 Paragr

What Is a Story?

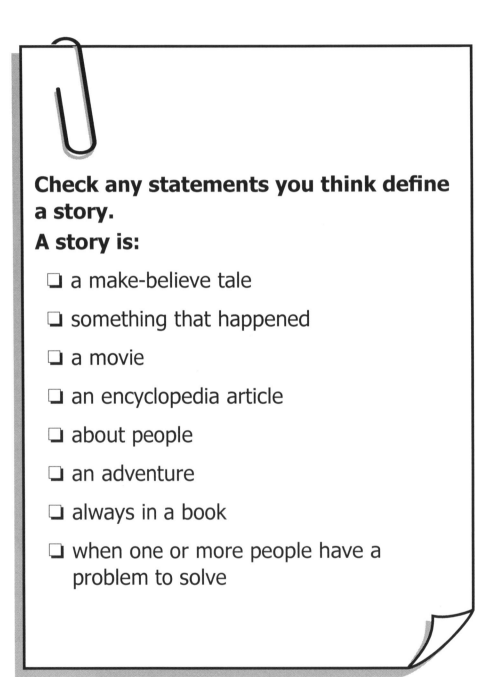

Check any statements you think define a story.

A story is:

❏ a make-believe tale

❏ something that happened

❏ a movie

❏ an encyclopedia article

❏ about people

❏ an adventure

❏ always in a book

❏ when one or more people have a problem to solve

Who Will Read My Story?

Objective

Students recall experiences they would like to share with peers, and then tell stories with their listeners' interests in mind.

Materials

- whiteboard or overhead projector and appropriate markers
- index cards, one per student

Opening

1. Draw a simple web on the whiteboard or overhead transparency, and write your name in the center circle. Talk through completing the web with the names of people who are important to you, such as a sister, cousin, or friend. Write the names of these people in the outer circles of the web.

2. Ask students to create a similar web with their names in the center circle and the names of people who are important to them. Suggest parents, grandparents, aunts, uncles, cousins, brothers, sisters, friends, coaches, favorite teachers, librarians, etc.

Directions

1. Explain that the people included on the students' webs represent people who might like to hear or read their stories.

2. Discuss what types of stories individuals listed on students' webs might like. For example, a friend might enjoy a funny story. A younger sibling might enjoy a story about animals. A favorite teacher might want to read a true story about something that happened in the student's life.

3. Have students think of stories they would like to tell friends or classmates.

4. Encourage them to consider the following questions:
   - What does my friend like that I also like?
   - What has happened to me that I would like my friend to know?
   - What experiences have I had that I wish my friend had been there for?

5. Have students write a few phrases about something they would like to share with classmates/friends.

6. Students can practice telling their stories to partners.

Closing

1. Give each student an index card. On their cards, students can draw a face to represent how their partners' stories made them feel. (*sad*, *excited*, *curious*, etc.) Remind students to show respect for their classmates' feelings.

2. Have them write sentences describing one thing they enjoyed about the stories.

Why Do People Write Stories?

Objective

Students complete sentence frames and correctly identify reasons why authors write stories.

Materials

- "Story Descriptions," page 10
- "Why Authors Write," page 9, one copy per student
- card stock or heavy paper for photocopying

Preparation

1. Prepare "Story Descriptions" by photocopying them onto card stock or heavy paper. Cut the descriptions apart. Each story description has a number.
2. When photocopying "Why Authors Write," fold paper under at dotted line to hide answers.
3. Post story description strips around the room.

Opening

1. Invite students to think about why they write stories.
2. Help students go beyond a "The teacher says I have to write a story" response by engaging them in a quick activity. Begin with one of the following statements and invite students to participate, one at a time, in quick succession.
   - The last time I told a scary story was when . . .
   - I like to tell funny stories to . . .
   - My friends and I take turns telling stories to each other when . . .
3. Have students complete the following sentence frame:
   I write stories because _____.
4. Have them turn and share their responses with partners. They will then share their partners' responses with the class, saying,
   (partner's name) writes stories because _____.

Directions

1. Continue a class discussion about the reasons to write stories.
2. Distribute copies of "Why Authors Write."
3. Have students walk around the room, identifying the story description that goes with each reason. Each student will write the number of a story description next to the appropriate author's reason on his or her paper.

Closing

1. Gather the posted "Why Authors Write" descriptions, read them aloud, and discuss them.
2. Have each student select one purpose he or she would like to try. Have them write one or two sentences to explain how they would put that purpose into practice.
   For example: I just learned about old growth forests. I would like to write a story that is set in an old growth forest.

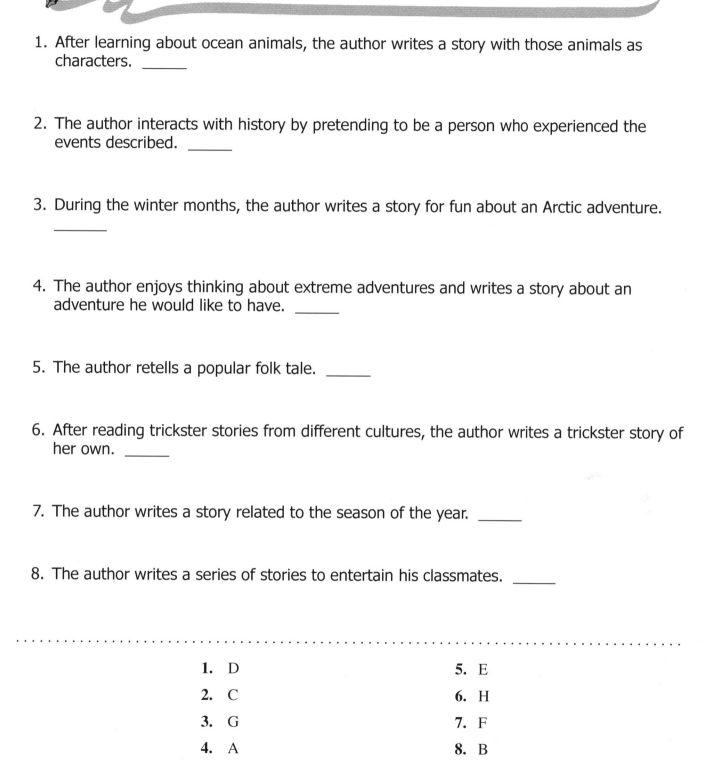

Why Authors Write

1. After learning about ocean animals, the author writes a story with those animals as characters. _____

2. The author interacts with history by pretending to be a person who experienced the events described. _____

3. During the winter months, the author writes a story for fun about an Arctic adventure. _____

4. The author enjoys thinking about extreme adventures and writes a story about an adventure he would like to have. _____

5. The author retells a popular folk tale. _____

6. After reading trickster stories from different cultures, the author writes a trickster story of her own. _____

7. The author writes a story related to the season of the year. _____

8. The author writes a series of stories to entertain his classmates. _____

. . . .

1.	D	**5.**	E
2.	C	**6.**	H
3.	G	**7.**	F
4.	A	**8.**	B

Story Descriptions

A. A bungee jumper's cord snaps, and he falls into a river below, but escapes with only cuts and bruises.

B. Cat and Monkey have many funny adventures.

C. A slave has blisters and insect bites.

D. A turtle loses his toy rubber duck and asks different ocean critters if they have seen it.

E. As they cross the road, three turtles hear a voice threatening to make them into a casserole.

F. A farmer builds scarecrows that do not keep the birds away.

G. Two penguins escape a mean polar bear by sliding on trash can lids off a cliff down into the ocean.

H. An ant tricks insects by taking them for a walk in a field and getting them lost.

What Kinds of Stories Are There?

Objective

Students will learn about different types of stories and think of examples of each, then create a group poster.

Materials

- "So Many Stories," page 12, one per student
- sample stories
- age-appropriate dictionaries, one per group or one per student
- poster board and appropriate markers, one set per group

Opening

Display the covers of familiar stories. Ask volunteers to describe in one or two words what kind of story each represents. Students may also indicate why they do or do not like a particular story. (*I like it because it's funny; I don't like it because it's scary.*)

Directions

1. Divide students into groups. Distribute "So Many Stories." Ask students to look up and write down the definition for each type of story in the dictionary and then write it in the space below the word(s). Students may also use an online dictionary to define words.

2. Group members can help each other think of an example for each type of story.

3. As time allows, have groups share their examples with the class.

4. Have each group choose three or four kinds of stories to illustrate on a poster. (You may wish to assign types of stories to groups to ensure each type is represented.) Groups will create a poster listing the types of stories they chose, along with an illustration and brief explanation of each.

Closing

Allow time for groups to share their posters. Display student posters in the classroom for future reference when students write their own stories.

So Many Stories

family (autobiographical)

    definition: _____

    example: _____

adventure

    definition: _____

    example: _____

mystery

    definition: _____

    example: _____

funny

    definition: _____

    example: _____

scary

    definition: _____

    example: _____

fantasy

    definition: _____

    example: _____

science fiction

    definition: _____

    example: _____

legend

    definition: _____

    example: _____

myth

    definition: _____

    example: _____

fairy tale

    definition: _____

    example: _____

folk tale

    definition: _____

    example: _____

fable

    definition: _____

    example: _____

How Do People Write Stories?

Objective

Given an introduction to basic components of a story and free writing, students will use a graphic organizer to describe the beginning, middle, end, and problem in a sample story scenario.

Materials

- "A Complete Story," page 16, one copy per student and one copy for display
- one slip of paper per student
- interactive whiteboard or overhead projector and appropriate markers
- sample picture books about writing stories, such as:
  Arthur Writes a Story by Marc Brown, Scholastic (1996)
  If You Were a Writer by Jean Lowery Nixon, Aladdin (1988)
- Additional Resources, page 48

Preparation

1. Prepare "A Complete Story" for classroom display on an interactive whiteboard or overhead transparency.

2. Determine an event or situation that happened in your school or community recently with which all students would be familiar.

Opening

1. Give each student a slip of paper. Ask them to write one sentence to answer the following question: "How do authors write a story?"

2. Collect the slips of paper, and read several responses anonymously.

3. If desired, share stories about the writing process using picture books, author biographical notes from classroom books, or "How Authors Write a Story" on page 48.

Directions

Part 1

1. Display "A Complete Story."

2. Tell students that all stories have a beginning, middle, and an end. Explain that the characters in stories find themselves in situations in which they face problems they must solve or obstacles they must overcome.

3. Talk through the concepts of beginning, middle, and end using the graphic organizer questions.
   - A story starts when something happens that makes the character(s) realize the problem.
   - In the middle, the characters try to solve the problem. They react to the situation in different ways.
   - At the end of the story, characters solve the problem or overcome the obstacle.

How Do People Write Stories? *(cont.)*

Directions *(cont.)*

Part 1 *(cont.)*

4. Write "WHAT IF?" in large letters on the whiteboard or overhead transparency. Explain that writers often figure out how the characters will react and what will happen next in the story by asking themselves, "What if?"

5. Introduce the concept of "free writing." Ask volunteers to describe the process of free writing. (*Write without stopping for a set amount of time, write without changing words, write what comes into your mind.*)

Part 2

1. Tell the class they will think about these aspects of writing a story with the following sample scenario.

   The principal saw a mouse in her office.

2. Guide students as they begin to think about the story.

3. Identify the main character(s): the principal, any students who are involved, etc. Write notes in the "beginning" box on the displayed graphic organizer. Ask students questions about the beginning of the story. Continue to add comments in the first box on the organizer.

4. As a class, discuss how the characters react to the situation. Write notes in the box labeled "middle" of the story. Ask questions to generate ideas about what the characters could do in the situation and how they could solve the problem. The class may discover the problem is not the mouse itself, but how the principal reacts to the mouse! (*For example, waving arms might cause books and papers to fall on the floor and grade reports might get mixed up.*) Ask "What if?" as needed to keep the discussion moving.

5. Finally, ask students how the characters solved the problem. How does the story end? Make notes in the last box on the graphic organizer.

Part 3

1. On the board or overhead transparency, write one sentence to describe an event or situation or problem that happened recently in your school or community.

2. Have students free write about the event or problem for 5–10 minutes. They will use this time to brainstorm everything they can remember about the event, who was involved, and what problem the character(s) had to solve, as well as how he/she/they solved the problem.

3. Distribute copies of "A Complete Story." Have students use their free-writing notes to complete the page, organizing their thoughts as to what will happen in the beginning of the story, what happens in the middle, and how the story ends.

How Do People Write Stories? *(cont.)*

Directions *(cont.)*

Part 3 *(cont.)*

4. Students will use these notes to write a complete story about the situation or event. Their stories will have at least three paragraphs: a beginning, a middle, and an end.

   - In the first paragraph, they will introduce the characters and the problem.

   - In the middle paragraph, the character will react to the situation and/or do some things to try to solve the problem.

   - In the last paragraph, the character(s) will solve the problem, and students should include a concluding sentence. (Remind students this is a good place to have a strong closing sentence for a paragraph.)

Closing

Provide an opportunity for students to share their stories, either with an "author's chair" in your classroom or by reading their stories to another class.

A Complete Story

Beginning	Middle	End

How does the story start?

Who is involved?

What is the problem?

How do the characters react in the situation?

What do they do?

What do the characters do to try to solve the problem?

How does the story end?

How is the problem resolved?

How do the characters overcome any obstacles?

It All Works Together

Objective

Students will brainstorm a variety of possible entries for given categories and participate in an oral storytelling experience.

Materials

- "Story Parts" game card, page 19, one per student, plus two per group and one for display
- "Sample Group Game Card," page 20, for teacher reference
- index cards or slips of paper, five per student
- chart paper and appropriate markers (optional)

Preparation

1. Enlarge game card for display.
2. On cards, slips of paper, or the board, prepare samples for students to match on display game card.

Opening

1. Display "Story Parts" game card. Explain each category.
   - Characters—people who are in a story
   - Setting of time—when the story happens
   - Setting of place—where the story takes place
   - Problem—an obstacle or challenge the character must overcome, something wrong he or she must solve
   - Actions—what characters do to solve problem, how they react in the situation
2. Read or show students the sample words or phrases from the Preparation section. Use only a few from each category to help students' thinking when they brainstorm their own category ideas.
3. Ask students to identify the proper category for each. Post samples on display chart if desired.

Directions

1. Divide the class into groups of four or five students each. Assign group roles as follows:
   - Reader
   - Checker
   - Recorder
   - Reporter

If a group has only three students, one person may fulfill the role of reader and checker. If there are more than four students per group, assign a Recorder 1 and Recorder 2.

It All Works Together *(cont.)*

Directions *(cont.)*

2. Groups will play a Categories game. Give each student a "Story Parts" game card. Students will have 10 minutes to write as many words/ideas in each category on their game cards as they can. (Ask students not to talk.)

3. When time is up, give each group two blank game cards, and have students then fulfill their group roles:

   • The **Reader** will read one group member's card at a time.

   • The **Recorder** will create one group category card that includes all student entries.

   • The **Checker** will cross out any duplicate entries.

   • The **Recorder** will then rewrite the group category card to include only the unique entries.

   • The **Reporter** will share the group's card with the class.

4. Display completed group cards for student reference.

5. Give each student five index cards or slips of paper. Have students label each card with one category title: characters, setting of time, setting of place, problem, actions.

6. Each student will select characters, settings, etc. from the shared class responses that he or she would like to include in a story. Have students write their ideas on the appropriate cards.

Closing

1. Allow students time to think of stories using the ideas on their cards.

2. Have students orally tell their stories to partners. Partners may give feedback to each other, expressing how well the storyteller incorporated each element of the story, including whether or not the story had a clear problem and resolution.

3. (Optional) Have students write out their stories on paper.

Story Parts Game Card

Characters	Setting of Time	Setting of Place	Problem	Actions

Sample Group Game Card

Characters	Setting of Time	Setting of Place	Problem	Actions (things a character does to solve a problem)
mail carrier	time of day (morning, noon, evening, night)	specific buildings	character loses something	seeking (look for lost item)
teacher	season of year (summer, fall, spring, winter)	house (cottage, mansion, cabin, houseboat, etc.)	someone gets sick	go get help
old man	day of week	park (neighborhood park, amusement park, National Park etc.)	character is in an accident or knows of someone in an accident	walk, go somewhere (how characters can react)
girl in a mall	specific holiday (Christmas, Thanksgiving, etc.)	forest	change of plans	help (someone who is sick or in an accident, resolve conflict)
person with shaggy hair		ocean	character wants to do something and cannot	run away
uncle		mountains	afraid of something/ overcoming fears	learn how to overcome fear
man who owns a boat		office (doctor, dentist, business, etc.)	conflicts—between character and siblings, parents, friends, teacher, coach, etc.	Any conflict-resolution practices your students use may also be included in stories.
		stores (specific)	character's friend moves away	talk (write letter to friend who moved, resolve conflict)
		community places (specific, e.g., restaurant, mall, movies)	any other anonymous problems your students face	talk to someone, ignore the problem, do something else

Who Am I?

Objective

Students will think about aspects of a provided character and write a class story about that character.

Materials

- "Character Questions," page 23, for teacher reference
- one or more sets of "dress up" clothes
- interactive whiteboard, overhead projector, or chart paper and appropriate markers

Preparation

1. Use the "Character Questions" on page 23 to create a character description.

Opening

1. Engage students in a game in which they try to guess the description of a character you have in mind. Have students ask questions about your character.

2. Write your answers to their questions on the board to help further guide students' questions and discussion.

3. Encourage students to form a mental picture of this person.

Directions

1. Explain that often in a story, one or more characters keep the story moving by what they do and how they react to things that happen to them, just as we do in real life as we go through each day.

2. Continue helping students develop a concept of character by asking a student volunteer to dress up in the clothing. As a class, give this "character" a name.

3. Ask students a series of questions about the character the volunteer represents.

- If (<u>name of character</u>) walks out the door, what will he/she see?
- Where will this person go?
- How will he/she get there?
- Why does (<u>name of character</u>) need to or want to go to that place?
- What will he/she do when they get there?
- What happens on the way there?
- How does this person react?
- What problems does (<u>name of character</u>) have?
- How will he/she solve the problem(s)?
- What will happen if . . . ?
- What happens when (<u>name of character</u>) gets where he/she is going?
- What else would you want to know about (<u>name of character</u>) to feel like you know this person?

Who Am I? (cont.)

Directions (cont.)

4. Use the student responses to write a class story. Have a volunteer write the first sentence or beginning of the story.

5. Ask another student what happens next to the character, or what the character does next in the story. That person may write the idea in a sentence to continue the story.

6. Continue until most have had a chance to participate, depending on time and number of students.

Closing

1. Read the class story together with the students. Ask:

- What did the character(s) do that surprised you?

- What did you learn about the character(s) that you didn't know when we started?

- How did the character(s) change during the story?

- How did the character(s) affect what happened in the story?

- How did they react to things that happened to them or around them?

2. As time allows, revisit the description you introduced in the Opening activity. Have students write a paragraph about one thing that character might do.

Character Questions

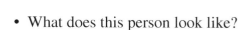

- What does this person look like?

- Does he or she have any special features, such as freckles, a knee brace, long curly hair, etc.?

- Where does he or she live? (town, city, country; what kind of house)

- How old is this character?

- What kind of pets, if any, does this person have?

- What does this character like to do?

- Does this person go to school or have a job?

- What does he or she like best in school? Or, what kind of job does he or she have?

- Who is in the character's family?

- How does he or she dress?

- What are the character's favorite toys?

- What are some other favorites, such as foods, sports, books, etc.?

- What is unusual about this character?

Add other characteristics relevant to your students.

Where and When?

Objective

Students will draw and describe a familiar setting in detail so a reader can establish the context for a story.

Materials

- colored pencils or crayons for each student
- white drawing paper, one piece per student

Preparation

Select a block in the neighborhood with which all students might be familiar. Physically preview the area, noticing details and taking notes for reference in class.

Opening

1. Review setting of time and place.

2. Discuss descriptive words that give the reader a mental picture.

3. Practice by having student volunteers describe the classroom as if the reader had never seen the room or as if describing it to a pen pal.

Directions

1. Introduce the block you previewed to the class.

2. Divide students into groups. Assign each group a different time setting, such as morning, noon, and night, or different seasons of the year. Each group will draw the predetermined neighborhood scene at their given time setting. Encourage students to include details, such as specific houses or other buildings, street names, landmarks (trees, bushes), and other features.

3. Ask students to place themselves in the scene doing something they have done before in that particular setting. To add interest, ask them what would happen if …? Or have students recall a conflict they resolved in that setting. For example: W*hen I was walking to school, an older student made fun of me and tried to take my lunch away.*

4. Have students write a short story, one to three paragraphs in length, about the scene, including the details from their picture.

Closing

Have students share their stories with partners. Students will draw stick figures or smiley faces for each statement below that is true for their partners' stories.
- I know where the story takes place.
- I can tell when the story happens.
- I have a mental picture of what happens in the story.
- The story seems real to me.
- The character faces a problem and solves it.

What Happened One Day

Objective

Given magazine pictures and a class brainstorming session, students will write beginning, middle, and ending paragraphs to create stories.

Materials

- magazine pictures of people, about a half dozen for display and one per group
- "Story Parts," page 20, completed group category game cards
- a pencil, one or more for demonstration
- whiteboard and appropriate markers (three different colors)

Preparation

Gather magazine pictures of people, or have students gather pictures prior to the lesson.

Opening

1. Review previous class discussions about how the main character in a story has a problem to solve or an obstacle to overcome.

2. Ask students what question they can ask themselves when they're writing a story to keep the action moving along. (*What if?*)

3. Introduce the word *plot*. Explain that plot is the main action and events in a story.

4. Review the concepts of what happens in the *beginning*, *middle*, and *end* of a story.

5. Display several magazine pictures of people. As a class, brainstorm one possible problem each person might have. (*If students have trouble, have them consider what might have gone wrong in that person's day, who he or she had a disagreement with and what it was about, what that person would like to do and why he or she cannot do it, etc.*)

6. Refer to group category cards as necessary for additional ideas.

Directions

Part 1

1. Conduct a simple demonstration to teach different actions characters might do in a story.

2. Ask three volunteers to come to the front of the room.

3. Hand the first student a pencil. Instruct the student to drop the pencil. Ask that person to react by saying something. *What would you say if you dropped your pencil?*

4. Hand a pencil to the second student. This student will also drop the pencil. Ask the student to show his or her reaction with gestures. *What expression will be on your face if you drop your pencil?*

What Happened One Day *(cont.)*

Directions *(cont.)*

5. The third student will also drop a pencil. Have this person show his or her reactions with movement. *What will you do after you drop the pencil? How will you move your hands or your feet?*

6. Explain that this is a very small picture of how characters can react and show action when they are faced with things that happen in a story.

   Write the three key types of action on the board, each word in a different color:

   speaking

   expressions or gestures

   movement

7. Encourage students to use one or more of these actions to show how characters react and what happens in the story.

8. Remind the class that as characters try to solve the main problem, they may encounter smaller problems or obstacles along the way.

Part 2

1. Divide students into groups of two to four students each. Give each group a magazine picture.

2. The group will work together to write one paragraph to tell the "beginning" of the story. Their paragraph should introduce the character(s), the problem or obstacle faced, and the setting in which the story takes place.

2. Have groups give their paragraphs and pictures to other groups. The second group will write a paragraph to tell the middle of the story. This paragraph will include different things the character(s) do to try to solve the problem.

3. Finally, groups will pass both paragraphs (beginning and middle) and magazine pictures to a third group. These students will write a paragraph to tell the end of the story. The character(s) should find a way to solve the problem. The reader should be satisfied that the conflict has been resolved in a way that makes sense and the story has ended. Encourage students to think of interesting, unusual, or unexpected ways to end their stories.

Closing

1. Conduct a class discussion on students' experience with the process of putting paragraphs into stories.

2. Have students write short journal entries describing what they learned about plot and how it works in a story.

3. Display compiled group stories for students to read as they have free time.

Who Said That?

Objective

Students will practice dialogue using sample dialogue and puppets, and match conversation snippets to appropriate characters.

Materials

- "Sample Dialogue Paragraph," page 28, one copy for display
- "Sample Problem Statements," page 29, one statement per pair of students
- "He Said, She Said," page 30, one per student
- audio story or video clip
- puppets, one per student, if possible; or use simple stick puppets

Preparation

1. Cue the audio story or video clip to a short dialogue segment.
2. Prepare "Sample Dialogue Paragraph" for class display.
3. Photocopy problem statements and cut them apart so each pair of students will have one statement.
4. When copying "He Said, She Said" for students, fold answers under at the dotted line.
5. If ready-made puppets are not available, have students draw pictures of friends, family members, or other characters from stories. Students can cut out the figures and tape them to wide craft sticks, paint stirrer sticks, or plastic spoons to make stick puppets.

Opening

1. Play the audio story or video clip dialogue segment.
2. Ask students what we call it when characters talk in a story. Introduce the word *dialogue*.

Directions

Part 1

1. Refer to the audio story or video clip. Discuss how the dialogue added to the story. Explain that characters talk in a story for a reason. Dialogue does many things:
   - shows what happens in the story
   - allows readers to get to know the characters
   - moves the story along

   Display the "Sample Dialogue Paragraph." Tell students that every time a different person speaks, a new paragraph begins. That's how we know that another character is speaking.

2. Pair students to work with partners. Give each pair of students a sample problem statement.

Who Said That? (cont.)

Directions (cont.)

3. Have students use puppets to practice dialogue as the "characters" try to solve the problem. If desired, have pairs take turns demonstrating for the rest of the class.

Part 2

1. Distribute copies of "He Said, She Said" to students.

2. Students will draw lines to match each statement with the person who might have said that statement.

Closing

Go over the matching statements together as a class. Discuss how each statement might contribute to the action in a story.

Sample Dialogue Paragraph

"Do you have your soccer shoes?" asked Cody's mom.

"Yes, mom, I have them." Cody slung his soccer bag over his shoulder and headed to the car.

"My mom thinks I can't remember anything," thought Cody as he tossed his bag into the car and slid into the other seat.

When they got to the Westfield Elementary soccer field, Cody wanted to run out to meet his friends.

"You forgot your water bottle." His mom opened her door to give Cody his water.

"Thanks," said Cody. So maybe he did forget things once in a while. It was nice to have a mom who made sure he had everything he needed. If his mom had not given him his water bottle, Cody would not have been able to practice.

"If you don't drink your water, you don't get to play," the coach always said. Cody drank a little water and headed out onto the field.

Sample Problem Statements

Hoshi draws a picture with her mother's new permanent marker and gets it all over her hands and arms, and she has a music/dance recital (band concert, piano recital, etc.) that evening.

- -

Devon's father goes away on a business trip and will be gone for two weeks. He misses his dad terribly, and his father will miss the All-Stars baseball game.

- -

On the way to school, older children chase Maahir. As he tries to escape, he runs through some bushes and tears the new coat from Grandmother.

- -

Brita's teacher has moved away. The new teacher explains math differently from the old teacher. Brita doesn't understand math, and every day she gets more confused. She doesn't know what to do.

- -

Alexis has stress fractures in both legs from running and playing basketball. Now she has a boot on one leg and an air cast on the other. She will miss practice and games during winter vacation.

- -

Colin goes to an amusement park with his best friends. He is scared to go on the biggest roller coaster.

He Said, She Said

1. "Did you find your lost library book?"	16-year-old girl
2. "When can you come over to play?"	third-grade teacher
3. "I'll take a sack lunch Friday for the company meeting."	11-year-old boy
4. "Class, Michaela's grandfather will come next week to talk to us about growing up on a reservation."	mother
5. "I traded my Xbox® for a computer."	man going to work
6. "I'm going to take the driver's test tomorrow."	7-year-old boy
7. "When I go to the paintball arena, I see all of my friends."	college student
8. "My niece is coming to celebrate her 28th birthday in three days."	school cook

. . . .

1. mother	5. college student
2. 7-year-old boy	6. 16-year-old girl
3. man going to work	7. 11-year-old boy
4. third-grade teacher	8. school cook

Building Suspense

Objective

Students explore possible actions, reactions, and resulting problems in a given story scene by playing a game.

Materials

- flashlight
- story book
- several pieces of long rope suitable for tug-of-war type game
- student stories from "What Happened One Day" lesson

Preparation

Review student stories from "What Happened One Day" lesson and identify specific actions, problems, or obstacles that can be used as one-line statements for the game.

Opening

1. Turn out one or more overhead lights. Hold a book in one hand, and shine the flashlight on the book. Ask a student to describe a time when he or she was reading a book and didn't want to put it down. Maybe he or she even kept reading after bedtime to find out what happened next in the story!

2. Ask students to give one word to describe the element in a story that makes readers want to keep on reading. (*suspense*)

3. Define suspense as an anxious, uncertain, or curious feeling caused by having to wait to see what happens.

Directions

1. Call two student volunteers to begin a game activity. The objective is for students to understand the many directions in which one story idea could go.

2. Have each student hold on to part of a rope.

3. Read something that happened in a story. Ask the first student what might happen next.

4. Encourage the other student to think of a *different* direction for the story; a *different* action the character could take.

5. Have two more volunteers come up. They each will stand next to one of the students holding the rope.

6. The two new students will hold the rope and take turns restating each action the first students suggested.

7. If desired, at each point write statements on cards to help students remember—but this may detract from the momentum.

Building Suspense *(cont.)*

Directions *(cont.)*

8. Have two more student volunteers join the game. Give the students a piece of the rope and have them state what might happen next in the story, after the action the second volunteers restated in #4, encouraging them to think of different directions the story might take.

9. Continue as long as there is enough rope and class interest.

Closing

1. Have students take one of the ideas expressed in the group activity and write a few sentences or a paragraph about what might happen next in the story. Encourage them to write something that will make the reader curious about what will happen next.

2. If time allows, have students trade papers with partners. After reading their partners' story continuations, they will write two or three questions they have about where the story will go from there.

A Character's Mood

Objective
Students will match actions to feelings on word cards, and write expressive journal entries.

Materials
- "Characters Feel … Characters Act," page 34, one per student

Opening
1. Ask students how they would define "mood." (*the way you feel*) Explain that the mood of a story is how it makes the reader feel.

2. As a class, list three or four feeling words on the board. (*happy, sad, mad*) For each word, have students brainstorm how a character in a story might act to show that feeling.

Directions

Part 1
1. Conduct a class discussion to expand on the idea of characters showing feelings by their actions. Ask:
   - How would we know a person in the story is afraid?
   - How do we know someone is feeling guilty?

2. Distribute copies of "Characters Feel … Characters Act."

3. Have students work with partners to think of one or more actions for each feeling to complete the chart.

Part 2
1. Have students think of stories they read recently. Ask them to think about how the stories made them feel. Model by thinking aloud if necessary:

   I read a fantasy about two kings who each wanted another kingdom to be on his side. The mean king stole something that had been hidden in the forest. I was upset he stole from the neutral kingdom, but curious to find out what he stole that would give him power over the good kingdom. I was happy that the good king won the battle.

2. Have students write journal entries describing how the stories they read made them feel. Encourage students to recall feeling words from the chart they completed with their partners.

Closing
1. Call on volunteers to explain how *mood* made a difference in the stories they read.

2. Create a class chart to list feeling words and related actions for student reference when they write their own stories. Use responses from the charts students completed with their partners.

Characters Feel... Characters Act

Describe an action that goes with each feeling by completing this sentence:

> When I'm (<u>feeling</u>), I (<u>action</u>).

For example, When I'm excited, I jump around.

Write the action word in the column next to each feeling word.

Feelings	Actions
excited	*jump around*
contented	
sad	
delighted	
grouchy	
sorrowful	
happy	
sleepy	
scared	
satisfied	
friendly	
frightened	
grieving	
afraid	
worried	
sympathetic	
mean	
cheerful	
compassionate	
peaceful	
calm	

Show, Don't Tell

Objective

The class will rewrite a story sample to show action instead of telling the story.

Materials

- "Jason's Pet," page 37, sample story for teacher reference
- "Jason's Pet Rewrite," below, sample for teacher reference
- interactive whiteboard or poster board and appropriate markers

Preparation

Prepare sample story for display on interactive whiteboard or overhead projector.

Opening

1. Call on one or two volunteers to tell about something that happened recently at school—in class, on the playground, at lunch, a school assembly, etc.

2. Invite two or three other volunteers to act out, or show, the same event. Ask students which version holds their interest more and why.

Directions

Part 1

1. Display the sample story. Read the story together as a class.

2. Go back over the story, one sentence at a time. Ask students to help you rewrite the story so it *shows action*, rather than *tells what happened*. You may wish to guide the discussion with the following questions:
   - How could we show that Jason is sad? What do people do when they are sad?
   - How can Dmitry offer to share his dog with Jason?
   - How does Jason's mother know he wants a pet?
   - How can dialogue (characters talking) show what happens in a story?
   - How could we include the five senses in this story?

3. Have three or four students act out the story.

Jason's Pet—Rewrite

Jason hung his head as he shuffled home from school.

"Why are you so down?" his friend Dmitry asked.

"I can't have a pet. They're not allowed in our apartment."

"Oh. You can share my dog!" Dmitry smiled. "Do you want to come over today and play with him?"

"No, but thanks anyway." Jason waved to Dmitry and walked the rest of the way home.

At home, Jason looked at his dog books. He didn't say much all afternoon.

"Why don't you think about a pet that doesn't take up much space and doesn't make noise? How about a pet plant or a pet rock?" his mother suggested.

A plant or a rock didn't sound like fun to Jason. He knew some people had cyber pets, but he didn't have his own computer, and it sounded too confusing.

Show, Don't Tell (cont.)

Directions (cont.)

Part 2

1. Use an interactive whiteboard or poster board to review how authors can use the principle of "show, don't tell" in their writing.

2. Write each of the following three points at each point of a triangle shape.

> Use actions to show how the characters feel.

> Include the five senses to show the action in the story.

> Include dialogue (characters talking to each other).

Closing

1. Discuss how students incorporated the five senses in the Opening activity when they related an event that happened at school.

2. Have students write one or more paragraphs describing the school event as a story. Remind them to refer to the triangle points to "show, don't tell."

Jason's Pet

(Sample Story)

Jason was sad because he wanted a pet. He couldn't have one because he lived in an apartment. His friend Dmitry said Jason could share his dog. Jason didn't think sharing a dog would be like having his own pet. His mother suggested he find a pet that didn't take up any space. She said it could be a plant or a rock. A plant or a rock didn't sound like fun to Jason. He knew some people had cyber pets. But he didn't have his own computer, and it sounded too hard. Jason's neighbor, Mr. Sully, worked for the humane society. Mr. Sully always had a story for Jason about the dogs and cats that needed good homes. Jason couldn't even help one animal!

One day Mr. Sully invited Jason to visit the humane society with him. He needed help and Jason was willing to go. Jason helped Mr. Sully clean cages and feed dogs. He took animals out into the yard. He enjoyed being with the dogs and playing with them. Mr. Sully asked Jason if he could come one or two days a week to help. After a few weeks, Jason borrowed a dog to take to school for Show and Tell. When he worked at the humane society, it felt almost like having his own pet!

Mapping a Story

Objective

Students will use a map graphic organizer to map out or plan a story.

Materials

- maps for display
- "Sample Story Maps," page 40
- "Champion Goalie," page 39, sample story for teacher reference
- colored pencils, pens, or highlighters

Preparation

1. Make one copy of "Wesley Creek School," the sample story map, for display.
2. Prepare another copy with the labels removed. (playground, office, classrooms, soccer field, big tree, etc.)

Opening

1. Display one or more maps. Ask students to describe how and why people use maps.
   - to get directions to a particular place
   - to find a particular object (such as a store)
   - to find a landmark (such as a river) or place (such as a city)
2. Ask how writers can map out a story for the same reasons.
   - to find (plan) the way from the beginning to the end of the story
   - to identify particular events that happen in a story, and in which order they occur
   - to give a story a sense of place—a visual/mental image for the reader

Directions

1. Display the sample map, "Wesley Creek School." Point out labels and discuss.
2. Review and list the basic story elements discussed in previous lessons. (*characters, setting of place, setting of time, plot/events that happen, problem that character has to solve, suspense/moments of "what if?"*)
3. Display the copy of the sample school map with the labels removed.
4. Work together as a class to map out a story.
5. First, map out the general story terms.
6. Then, map out a specific story by talking through the sample story, "Champion Goalie."
7. Give each student a copy of the sample story map without labels. Display the class copy with the story elements included on the map.
8. Have students refer to the general story terms map to create their own story maps with specific items for each element.

Mapping a Story *(cont.)*

Closing

Students will use the story map they created to write a complete story.

Champion Goalie

(sample story to map out)

Towering maple trees surrounded the park. Seth barely noticed the colorful leaves as he ran on to the soccer field. He blocked a short pass from Ivan and joined the team as they ran a practice drill before the big game. Their opponents, the Wolves, had not lost any games yet. Seth played goalie. He wanted to block every shot the Wolves tried to make.

The whistle blew. Seth and his teammates hustled into position. Ivan blocked the opening kick by the Wolves and passed it up to a forward. The Wolves' midfielder intercepted it. He sent the ball back down the field towards Seth. The ball hit a rough clump of grass and bounced off the ground.

Seth's foot slipped on the mud as he leaned forward to catch the ball. It stopped just short of the goalie box. Seth scrambled to kick it back up field. One of the Wolves beat him to it. The player kicked the ball in a desperate attempt to make a goal before the end of the half. His feet still sliding on the mud, Seth lunged and landed on the ball, face down. The whistle blew. No score! Seth had held them so far.

Sample Story Maps

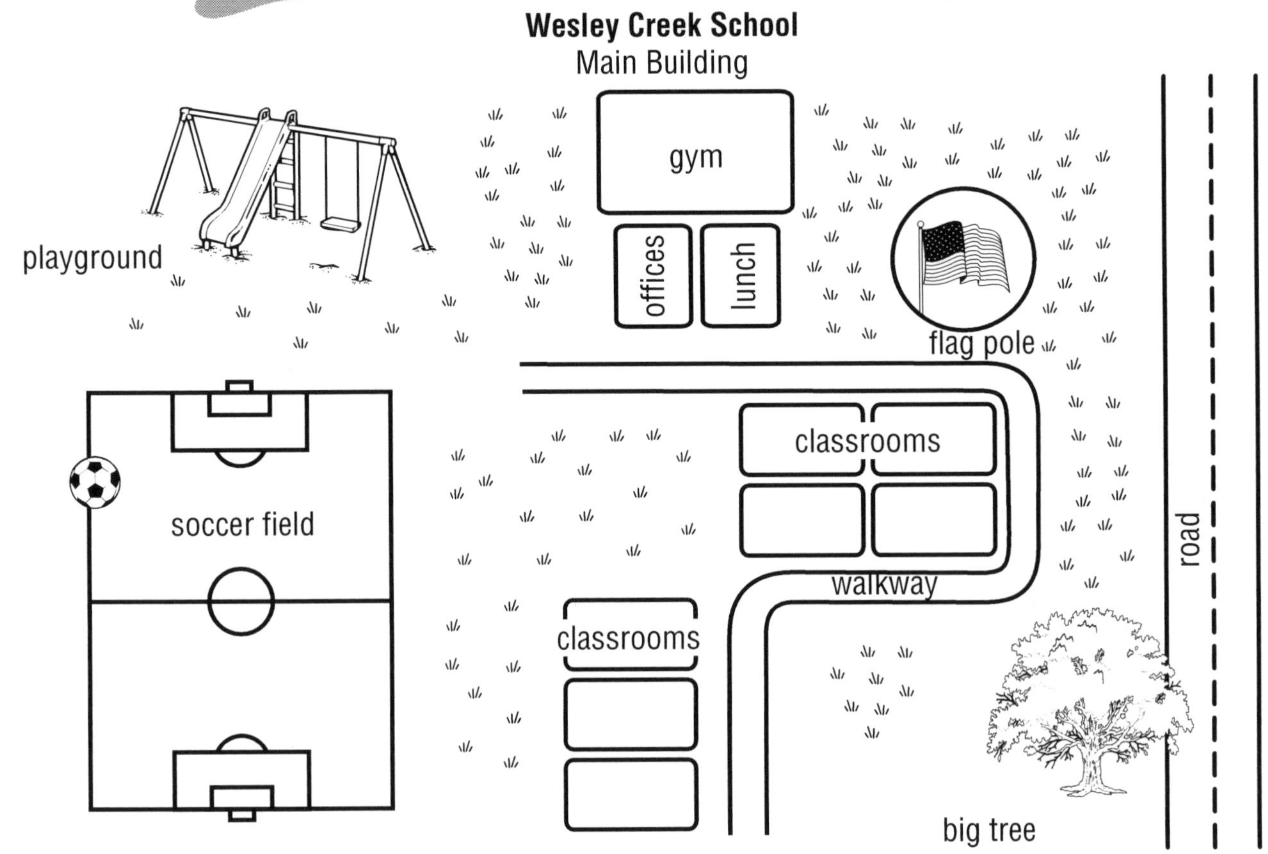

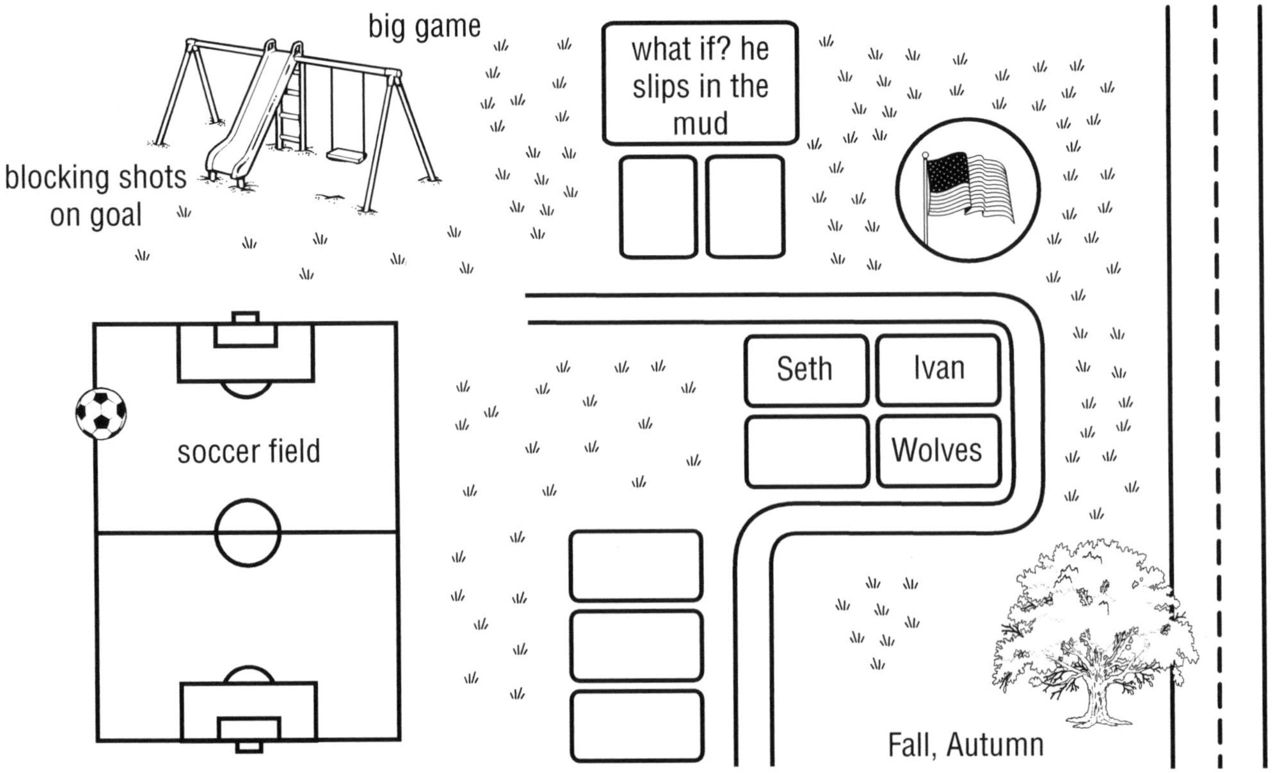

Wesley Creek School
Main Building

playground

gym

offices

lunch

flag pole

classrooms

walkway

road

soccer field

classrooms

big tree

---

big game

blocking shots on goal

what if? he slips in the mud

soccer field

Seth

Ivan

Wolves

Fall, Autumn

Our Adventures

Objective

Materials

- paper or labels to identify objects as needed
- stuffed animals (optional)

Preparation

Set up an obstacle course on the playground, in the gym, or in the classroom.

Opening

1. Create a class web using the word *adventure* for the center. Have students brainstorm characteristics and features of an adventure they might take. Include possible locations and conflicts or problems they might encounter.

2. Show students the obstacle course. As a class, list the obstacles, and give each obstacle a "label" indicating what it might represent in an adventure setting. Encourage students to incorporate ideas from the class web or based on the specific types of adventures that interest them.

   - a *bridge* on a playground structure could be a *bridge* across a river or a canyon that a character has to cross to reach a destination—perhaps something dangerous or uncertain awaits on the other side

   - a *cave* could be under a playground structure platform or behind a door—the character does not know what is in the cave, or perhaps he/she meets someone in the cave

   - a *ladder, slide, or rope* in the gym, or *beanbag* in the classroom might represent a mountain—perhaps the character encounters hardships climbing the mountain

   - *stuffed animals or other figures* could represent any animals or people the character encounters who keep him/her from doing what he/she wants to do

Directions

1. Have one pair of students at a time navigate the obstacle course. Remind them to imagine they are in the scene or location of their chosen adventure. They will take turns taking notes about which difficulties they face and how they overcome any challenges.

2. While the rest of the class waits their turn, they may draw pictures of their imagined adventures, take notes about the character(s) who will be in their stories, or think of problems their character(s) must solve.

3. Discuss with students the concept of a "narrative" story. Explain that as they write their stories, they will put into practice what they have learned about putting events in a logical order and making a story seem real.

Closing

1. Have each student write an adventure story.

2. Ask students to illustrate their stories.

3. Students may present their stories to the class in an Author's Chair or other setting.

Editing My Story

Objective

Students will practice editing their stories in centers.

Materials

- student dictionaries
- grammar reference materials
- colored pencils
- "A Complete Story" (graphic organizer on page 16) from "How Do People Write Stories?" lesson
- word processing work stations (computers with word processing software or interactive whiteboard)
- scissors, tape, plain white drawing paper (optional)
- "Editing Checklist," page 44
- story maps, graphic organizers

Preparation

1. Set up several student work centers around the room. Label the centers as follows:
   - Spelling
   - Grammar
   - Punctuation and Capitals
   - Paragraphs
   - Story Structure
   - Story Elements

2. Place tools in each center:
   - Spelling—student dictionaries and relevant spelling lists
   - Grammar—any classroom posters or other related reference materials
   - Punctuation and Capitals—colored pencils
   - Paragraphs—graphic organizers, story maps
   - Story Structure—copies of "A Complete Story" graphic organizer
   - Story Elements—story maps

3. Have students select a completed story they wrote during one of the previous lessons. Photocopy student stories.

Opening

1. Review the term "editing." Ask students what they will need to look for in their writing to edit their stories—to make the writing correct or make the story better.

2. Create a class chart if you don't already have one.

Editing My Story (cont.)

Opening (cont.)

3. Introduce the idea of using "tools" to edit. Have students brainstorm tools they might use to edit their writing. (*dictionaries, a friend or teacher, colored pencils to circle things, grammar checker, an editing checklist*)

Directions

1. Keep a copy of each student story. Give each student a copy of his or her story.

2. Point out the centers and labels to the class. Explain that students will rotate through the centers, editing stories they have written.

3. Distribute copies of the "Editing Checklist." Suggest that as students visit each center, they check off the particular aspects of the story they edited at that center.

4. Randomly assign students to a rotation schedule in which a few students visit each center at a time. If you have too many students for all to work at centers at once, students may begin to edit their work at their desk while they wait, or work on completing another story.

5. As students visit each center, they should use the tools available to focus on that particular aspect of editing their story.

6. Collect student's edited stories. Make anonymous copies of the original and edited student stories.

Closing

1. Give each student anonymous copies of a classmates' original and edited stories.

2. Have students read the two versions of the story and complete the following sentence frames:

   - I can tell the author edited _____.

   - The edited story is better because _____.

   Give examples.

   - *I can tell the author edited the spelling because some hard words are spelled correctly.*

   - *The edited story is better because the author rearranged two paragraphs so the action happens in an order that makes sense.*

Editing Checklist

❏ I spelled all the words I know correctly. I used a dictionary to check words I don't know.

❏ I used nouns and verbs correctly in my writing.

❏ My writing has complete sentences.

❏ Every sentence has an ending punctuation mark—a period, a question mark, or an exclamation point.

❏ I checked to make sure I used commas and apostrophes correctly.

❏ Every sentence begins with a capital letter.

❏ Names begin with capital letters.

❏ Each new idea has a new paragraph.

❏ Paragraphs are indented

❏ My story has a beginning, middle, and an end.

❏ Events in the story happen in order.

❏ My characters seem like real people.

❏ My reader can tell where and when my story takes place.

❏ My characters have a problem to solve or an obstacle to overcome, and they solve the problem.

❏ I use action words and sensory details to make the story seem real.

Writing for Publication

Objective

Students will brainstorm ways they can publish their work, including preparing it for publication, and presenting it in some way.

Materials

- samples of published student work. (student magazines, bound collections of student work in books from the school or class library, posters, etc.)
- interactive whiteboard, word-processing software with ability to display for the class, or overhead projector
- materials for students to illustrate their work
- audio-visual equipment (optional)
- "I Could Be Published," page 47

Preparation

Gather available illustrative and presentation materials as necessary for your students.

Opening

Introduce the word *publish* by giving students clues and having them guess the word. Use these sample clues:

- to produce a story so someone will buy it
- to bring printed words before the public
- to share your story
- to bind your work into a book
- to submit writing to a magazine that agrees to print it

Directions

Part 1

1. Have students brainstorm ways they could be published. Suggest they start with one of these statements:
   - *I wish. . .*
   - *Wouldn't it be nice if. . .*
2. Encourage them to think beyond what they think would be logically possible. List students' ideas on the board. For example:
   - *I wish I could write a book.*
   - *Wouldn't it be nice if my story was accepted by a magazine?*
   - *I wish all my friends would read my story!*
   - *I wish I could be a famous author.*
   - *Wouldn't it be nice if my story was made into a movie?*
3. As a class, group main ideas into categories (such as magazine, wide audience, movie, etc.).

Writing for Publication *(cont.)*

Directions *(cont.)*

Part 1 *(cont.)*

4. Have students work in small groups of three or four to expand the thinking and brainstorming process for one specific category. Encourage them to think specifically *how* their stories could be published in this way. See "I Could Be Published" for ideas.

Part 2

1. Discuss with students what it means to "write for publication."

2. Show samples of "published" student work. Ask students what they notice about the work. (*It is in a format that is easy to read—typed or neatly written. All the words are spelled correctly. Sentences begin differently and are various lengths. The paragraphs make sense. It may have illustrations.*)

3. Use an interactive whiteboard, word processing software, or a sample created for an overhead projector to demonstrate margins, indenting paragraphs, and other basic formatting relevant to your students' abilities and publishing possibilities.

4. Have students work with the stories they edited previously. They may print them neatly and add illustrations, or use word-processing and other software to "publish" their work.

Closing

1. Help students select a publishing option from those discussed in class that fits their particular stories.

2. Provide illustration materials, access to audio-visual equipment, or other resources as needed; or arrange for students to share their work publicly (school assembly, parent night, nursing home, etc.).

I Could Be Published!

- Post your story to the class blog or website.
- Submit to specific magazines that publish children's work.
- Create a class magazine to distribute to parents or other classes.
- Work with the media center and create a movie of a story to show to classmates/peers.
- Read work at a school assembly or parent night.
- Create a book, bind it with a long arm stapler or binding machine, and add it to the classroom or school library.
- Include your story with a greeting card to a friend or family member.
- Perform your story with puppets for your classmates or another class.
- Check with a community center to learn about available options for student work displays, for example—the public library, a locally owned restaurant, etc.

Additional Resources

How Authors Write a Story (use with "How Do People Write Stories?" lesson, page 13)

"I usually start with a seed of a story, then move on to thinking about the character who fits that seed. (This often takes time.) I try to create the character who will get the most out of the conflict or challenge in the story. I think about how the character is going to change during the story, and I sketch out about three important scenes. I know how the story will begin and end, though those can change as I write. Then I sit down and start writing, giving myself permission to change what I've planned to fit the story that unveils as I write."—Cindy Kane Trumbore (used with permission)

"Whenever I have an idea, I put it down on a large index card. As I develop the story with plot ideas, scenes, and characters, I write them on the card. I approach a story or book in one of two ways. Sometimes the story comes and I feel as if I'm running after the characters to write down their story. Other times, I am not sure of the details of a story idea. This is when I create outlines of my characters and of the story. Now I have an idea where the story needs to go, even if it changes as I write."— Kathryn Lay (**www.kathrynlay.com**) (used with permission)

I saw a bumblebee in a garden and it gave me an idea for a story. Pockets magazine was the only magazine at the time that would accept a talking animal story. I wanted to put it in book form, but I didn't get around to it for awhile. I sat down and wrote it quickly, knowing how to tell it and what to say. —Elsie Larson (used with permission)

Made in the USA
Coppell, TX
07 October 2021